250 LIFEHACKS

FoR YoUNG AUTISTIC ADULTS

Your Guide to a Simpler Life

PETER VERMEULEN

In collaboration with the ambassadors of "strengthmakers *in* autism"

illustrations by Marloes De Vries

250 LIFEHACKS FOR YOUNG AUTISTIC ADULTS

All marketing and publishing rights guaranteed to and reserved by:

(817) 277-0727
fhautism.com

Text © 2025 Peter Vermeulen
Illustrations © 2025 Marloes De Vries

All rights reserved, including those for text and data mining, AI training, and similar technologies.

No part of this product may be reproduced in any manner whatsoever without written permission of Future Horizons, Inc., except in the case of brief quotations embodied in reviews or unless noted within the book.

Original edition published and licensed by Pelckmans Uitgevers nv (pelckmans.be)

ISBN: 978-1-963367-42-3

FOREWORD

The book you are holding in your hands now contains about 250 tips and tricks for a simpler life with autism. However, that doesn't mean an easy life. Because if you have autism, life is always a bit more challenging than for people without autism.

In this book you will find the twenty biggest challenges for people with autism. You will read what they can do themselves to tackle these challenges and also what their environment can do. This book is primarily written **for adults with autism**, and it is also aimed at their friends, neighbors, partners, parents and employers. By reading about the challenges and the accompanying tips, people without autism can also gain a better insight into what people with autism struggle with, where these challenges come from, and especially how they can help and support. If you are someone with autism, give this book to the people who are important to you, or read it together. Talk about the challenges and the tips.

Because that is where autism-friendliness starts: talking to each other about how things can be made easier and simpler.

This book is not just written *for* people with autism. It was also written together *with* people with autism. Nothing about us without us, that is what autistic people ask. And rightly so. The twenty challenges and all the tips in this book were developed through meetings with people with autism, specifically ambassadors of Strengthmakers *in* Autism, an organization that strives for full inclusion of people with autism. At the back of this book, the ambassadors introduce themselves.

Although my name is on the cover of this book, I have merely collected, organized, written down, and—where necessary—provided additional explanations for all their experiences, ideas, tips, and suggestions.

I was just the pen that put the ideas of people with autism on paper. It was a privilege to get insight into how they deal with the challenges that autism brings and how they often come up with solutions themselves.

Even after working with people with autism for over thirty-five years, I still learn so much from them. I deeply appreciate their insights and the many gripping—and sometimes humorous—stories they shared in our meetings. And I am proud of the end result: a practical book *for* and by people *with* autism.

Although this book is about the difficulties and challenges faced by people with autism, and the explanations are grounded in recent scientific insights, we have made every effort to present everything in a clear and light-hearted manner.

It is a misconception that people with autism have no sense of humor. That's why you'll find the delightful cartoons by Marloes De Vries in this book, along with playful tips, humorous exaggerations, and even metaphors and expressions. For some, this book may be a bit too simple and light-hearted. I would like to refer them to the many scientific books and books on autism for professionals. If, on the other hand, you find certain parts of the text difficult to understand—the explanation of autism at the beginning of this book is quite tough—then ask someone from your environment to read along and clarify where necessary.

While it is possible to read this book from cover to cover, you don't have to. If you want to skip the explanation of autism at the beginning of the book, feel free to do so. You can go straight to the super tips in the introduction or to any of the twenty challenges. Consider the table of contents as an à la carte menu, where you can pick and choose what interests you.

I want to thank in particular Pilar Peigh and her daughter Abigail for their help in getting the original Flemish version properly translated into English. As experts in the field, their assistance was invaluable.

I wish you much reading pleasure and inspiration.

Peter Vermeulen

INTRODUCTION

WHAT IS AUTISM?

Autism is the name of a group of behavioral characteristics that result from a brain that deals with the outside world and the internal world (one's own body) in an atypical way. Scientists have studied these behavioral characteristics and brought them together in the diagnostic criteria for autism.[1] The following are the characteristics:

Persistent difficulties with social communication and interaction. This is evident from difficulties with social-emotional reciprocity, such as ping-ponging in conversations and the balance of give and take in relationships. It is also evident from difficulties in understanding and using non-verbal communication, such as reading facial expressions. People with autism may also find it difficult to enter into, maintain, and understand relationships, such as making and keeping friends. Or they cannot distinguish well between different types of relationships and then, for example, deal with a manager in too familiar a way or with colleagues in too formal a way.

Restricted, repetitive patterns of behavior, restricted interests and activities. This is often seen in restricted, fixated interests that are unusually intense or narrowly focused. For example, people with autism may become preoccupied with a particular/singular topic or frequently want to talk about the same subject. They may also over- or under-react to sensory stimuli, or show an unusual interest in sensory aspects of the environment. Repeating certain movements or actions and having difficulty with new, unexpected things or unpredictable changes are also common characteristics of autism.

---

1. The official term is *autism spectrum disorder*. Due to the recent evolution in looking at autism from the perspective of neurodiversity, we opt for the more neutral term *autism*. Autism can manifest itself very differently in behavior, which is why we use the term autism for a broad spectrum of behaviors. There are differences in preference in language use: either *identity first* (autistic people) or *person first* (people with autism). That is why we use both terms. But we usually use *people with autism*, because that is often what they prefer in Flanders.

In addition to these core characteristics of autism, there are two additional criteria for a diagnosis of autism:

The described behavioral characteristics must be present from early childhood. This does not mean that they are always recognized at this young age. It does mean that you cannot develop autism at a later age. Because gifted people in particular can camouflage and compensate for their autism well, it sometimes happens that the diagnosis is only made in adulthood. Autism is not always (immediately) noticeable, especially during brief or casual interactions.

The characteristics must lead to significant difficulties in key areas of life, such as work, communication, leisure time, and often eating and sleeping.

Although you see these behavioral characteristics in all people with autism, you can't really make a list of specific autistic behaviors. The concrete way in which the difficulties in social communication and interaction manifest themselves can be very different. For example, there are autistic people who are very reserved in social contact and even avoid contact. But there are also those who very actively seek social contact, although sometimes in an awkward or even unpleasant way. And while all people with autism react unusually to certain sensory stimuli, their sensory profile is unique. For example, not all autistic individuals are super sensitive to sound or are bothered by touch.

All this to say, there is no such thing as typical autistic behavior. Autistic people have many unique characteristics beyond their autism, and the way these characteristics present varies from person to person.

Autism affects one in one hundred people. You often see higher numbers, especially on the internet, but you should take them with a grain of salt. Autism is not more common than it used to be, but the diagnosis is made more often. This has to do with several things:

- Society has become more complex. Increasing demands are being made on flexibility and social and communication skills, which means that people with autism who could function in the fixed structures of a hundred years ago, can no longer do so.

- There is much more knowledge about autism than a few decades ago. The characteristics of autism are more widely known, and as a result people are more likely to express a suspicion of autism.

- The image, or stigma, of autism is no longer as extremely negative as it was in the previous century. There is also increasing openness to neurodiversity, the understanding that there is wide variation in how brains work.

A BRAIN THAT WORKS DIFFERENTLY

The behavioral characteristics of autism are the result of a brain that works differently from a "neurotypical" brain. Autism is not located in one specific place in the brain. Autism is mainly in how that brain processes information.

To help us respond to the world quickly and efficiently, our brains have learned not to wait until they have gathered all the information about our current situation, but to anticipate that situation. Our brains make predictions about what is coming, so that we don't have to process all the information (What do we see? What do we hear? Who else is here? Where are we?) before we can respond.

For example, if you are crossing a sidewalk when the pedestrian light is green, your brain expects the light to turn red, possibly before you even reach the other side.

That anticipation makes sure that all your muscles are ready to accelerate as soon as the light turns red. That is more efficient than only kicking in when it has turned red (i.e., "Aha, the traffic light is changing color! What color is this and what should I do now?").

Our brain is constantly predicting. And that happens based on the knowledge it has gathered from previous experiences. For example, the brain has knowledge about traffic lights and knows, among other things, that traffic lights usually do not wait to change color until you have reached the other side of the street. Your brain has also learned that people do not always respect the rules and will dare to cross at a red light, knowing it is not allowed, but that is okay as long as no cars are coming.

Autistic brains, like other brains, also want to be prepared for what is coming. Therefore, they also predict. But unlike non-autistic brains, they are *very precise* in their predictions, and the knowledge they base this on is absolute and less context-sensitive.

It is this way of thinking that truly characterizes autism. Autistic people can differ greatly in their behavior, but what they all have in common is absolute thinking. Their ideas about the world are linear (something can only have one meaning), precise, and detailed, while the world is very relative. A red light does not always mean "stop." What is an appropriate gift for a friend, what is collegiality, what you talk about with the neighbors, what is "good enough" in a task, and what is an appropriate comment are all relative and context-dependent. This leads to a lot of confusion, frustration, and misunderstandings in autistic brains. A world without absolute rules is a world full of ambiguity and unpredictability. That is the core of autism: uncertainty.

The typical thinking style of the autistic brain leads not only to the already mentioned behavioral characteristics of autism (difficulties in social connections, communication, and responding to the environment), but also to other characteristics that we often see in autistic people, such as difficulties in monitoring physical needs and energy balance, sleep problems, stress, and anxiety.

THE CHALLENGES OF LIVING WITH AUTISM

Autism, therefore, brings with it many challenges. Together with a group of ambassadors of Strengthmakers *in* Autism, we selected twenty challenges that are important for many (young) adults with autism. Because we speak of an autism spectrum, it is possible that certain challenges in this book pose few or no difficulties for you.

Whether something is a challenge for you or not has not only to do with your autism but also with all kinds of other factors. For example, in addition to autism, your personality also plays a role. Extroverted people with autism may find parties or having a conversation less difficult than introverted people with autism. For some people with autism, conversations move too fast, for others, too slow.

The reverse is also possible: you may be dealing with challenges that did not make it onto the list of twenty. If that's the case, this book can also offer you tips and tricks for those challenges: many life hacks can be used for multiple challenges and in multiple contexts, such as at work or in the family.

TIPS FOR THE PEOPLE AROUND YOU

Many tips in this book require you to notice your body's signals in a timely and accurate manner. This is not easy for people with autism. Many of them find it difficult to keep their finger on the pulse, for example when it comes to their energy balance, their stress level, or clearing their head in time. (The technical term is *interoception*, reading what's happening inside your body.)

If this is also the case for you, it is useful to activate additional antennas and ask trusted people around you to help monitor your "pulse."

There are also limits to what you as a person with autism can achieve yourself. This applies to everyone: no one is completely independent. No one can do everything on their own. We all need others to survive. That is why this book not only contains tips for what you—as a person with autism—can do, but also tips for how others can help you with every challenge. An understanding environment in which people try to be autism-friendly can make life with autism a lot easier.

If you choose to involve others in the tips in this book, then it is useful to read these tips together and discuss them. Above all, agree on whether you want others to take the initiative to help you or not. Many adults with autism do not want to be a burden to others and therefore do not always spontaneously ask for help. If you are one of them, ask others to take the initiative by asking you how they can help if they think you are having a hard time with something.

Asking is important, because people—with the best intentions—all too quickly start making assumptions about someone else's needs and abilities and perhaps do things that do not help you at all or are not necessary for you. On the other hand, others cannot always see what can help you. That's why it's best to let others know what you need or ask if they can help you. For this reason, as you read through this book, you will often see the words *ask* and *tell* under "What Others Can Do."

HOW DO YOU USE THIS BOOK?

This book contains more than two hundred tips—quite a lot. You don't have to follow or try all the tips. The intention is not for you to read this book from cover to cover. Browse through it.

We suggest that you start with a challenge that is important to you, but perhaps not the biggest challenge. No one would expect a non-runner to run a marathon with one day of training. It would be a failed (painful) attempt, and perhaps cause that person to never run again (or at least for a while). This book certainly doesn't want to give you (another) failure experience. Start with the tips that could be good for you and have a big chance of success. Resilience is like muscle strength: you build it up gradually.

You will find that some challenges are related, such as surviving a party, having a conversation, and dealing with sensory overload. If that's the case, you'll see a link to tips in another challenge.

If a suggested tip doesn't work for you, try something else. Not all tips work for everyone. That's why there are multiple tips for each challenge.

It is also possible that a tip will only work for a while. If and when that happens, it may be a good idea to hit pause on that tip or think of a variation.

Don't look at this book as a magic wand that will solve all your problems once and for all, but as a collection of small, practical suggestions that can make life with autism a little easier. Life will never be completely easy and simple. The reality is, life isn't always easy and simple for anyone.

This book is a self-help book. Dealing with the challenges that autism brings with it starts with you: things that you can do, with or without the help of the people in your immediate environment (your partner, friends, family, colleagues, neighbors). But sometimes that is not enough. Sometimes people with autism face so many challenges, or challenges that are very big, that they cannot cope without professional help. If you notice that the tips in this book do not make any difference, seek professional help.

FIVE SUPER TIPS

Before we get to the challenges and the associated lifehacks, let's review an all-encompassing toolbox with five recommendations (super tips) that can help you with many different challenges.

❶ TALK TO OTHERS ABOUT YOUR CHALLENGES

Are you facing a challenge that is causing you stress, making you insecure, or giving you the feeling that you are failing? If so, then talk about it with people around you that you trust. There's a good chance others may not always see that something is difficult for you, as they do not have autism themselves. Also, it's virtually impossible to look directly into someone's mind and know what they are experiencing. Others may find it challenging to understand you or your needs, if they are not aware of what is difficult for you. So talk about it. Always remember, two heads know more than one, and together you may come up with more and better solutions.

❷ VISUALIZE THE AGREEMENTS WITH YOURSELF

It's been said, "The road to hell is paved with good intentions." Chances are, many of the tips in this book will appeal to you, and you will feel like using them. Often, good intentions do not get further than, "This is what I want to do!" To prevent intentions from fizzling out, make concrete agreements with yourself about the tips you want to try. What are you going to do? When, where, how, how often, and for how long will you try the tip? Here's an example: "After a busy day at work, I will sit in the living room and listen to five songs from my Spotify relaxation list." This action step is important to do because we often tend to forget even the best intentions. (After that busy day, it does not occur to you to open your song list.) It is extremely useful to create reminders that you can literally see. Hang Post-its up, have reminders appear on your smartphone screen, put things in sight that remind you of a tip. For the example agreement above: hang the logo of your music streaming service where you hang your coat when you get home, or on the bathroom door. (You'll definitely pass that one.)

③ KEEP BREATHING

Most of the challenges shared in this book involve stress. There are many different ways to de-stress, but one technique that almost anyone can learn and easily use in different contexts is abdominal breathing with long exhalation. Inhale (through your nose) for 4 counts, hold for 5 counts, and exhale (through your mouth) for 6 counts. Can't hold your breath? Then leave that part out and breathe in (4 counts) and out (6 counts). It is important that you breathe out longer than you breathe in, and that you breathe from your belly and not from your chest. When you breathe in, your belly expands. When you breathe out, you push the air out of your lungs from your belly. You can find numerous videos on the internet that show you how it works. If you regularly do this relaxation, breathing consciously for a few minutes, it helps remove the stress hormones from your body. Even if you are overstimulated, this breathing can help you calm down quickly.

④ MOVE

Mens sana in corpore sano (Latin for "a healthy mind in a healthy body")

The Romans already knew in the first century AD that physical exercise is not only good for your physical health but also for your mental resilience. Physical exercise helps clear your head and makes your brain stronger. It enhances your cognitive abilities and invigorates your thinking. Plus, it becomes a lot easier to regulate your emotions. So, plan regular exercise activities. You don't have to train for a triathlon or a Himalayan mountain climb. It could look like taking the stairs instead of the elevator. Park your car a bit further away and walk the last part. Start each day with a dance. Take a walk in the park or the forest at least once a week. These are just a few examples. If you find it difficult to get excited for a sport or exercise, try the 1-2-3 rule: count out loud from 1 to 3 and then start the exercise.

⑤ FIND SUPPORTERS

You may discover that applying these tips on a continual basis is difficult. Find supporters who will encourage you to apply the tips or problem solve with you on what to do if a tip does not work exactly as you thought, planned, or hoped. Ask people to partner with you in areas where you need a little extra encouragement (for example, walking together, drawing up a weekly menu together, etc.). Or involve people in reminding you of agreements you made with yourself (for example, a colleague who reminds you to take a break).

20 CHALLENGES

These are the twenty challenges that are addressed in this book:

1. MONITORING AND MAINTAINING ENERGY BALANCE 15
2. SETTING BOUNDARIES AND DARING TO SAY NO 21
3. DEALING WITH A FULL HEAD 25
4. PLANNING AND ORGANIZING 29
5. DEALING WITH YOUR OWN EMOTIONS 33
6. DEALING WITH THE EMOTIONS OF OTHERS 39
7. OVERCOMING THE FEAR OF DISAPPOINTING OTHERS 43
8. MAKING CHOICES AND DECISIONS 47
9. SWITCHING FROM ONE THING TO ANOTHER 51
10. DEALING WITH UNPREDICTABLE EVENTS 55
11. DEALING WITH SENSORY OVERLOAD 61
12. HAVING CONVERSATIONS 67
13. BUILDING AND MAINTAINING CLOSE RELATIONSHIPS 73
14. SURVIVING PARTIES 79
15. SLEEPING WELL 85
16. ENJOYING MEALS 91
17. DEALING WITH LOSS 95
18. BOOSTING YOUR NEGATIVE OR LOW SELF-ESTEEM 101
19. BEING YOURSELF IN CONNECTION WITH OTHERS 107
20. ACCEPTING YOURSELF 113

MONITORING AND MAINTAINING YOUR ENERGY BALANCE

Nothing is absolute in the world. Everything is relative and context-dependent. A world with ever-changing and unpredictable rules demands an enormous amount of energy from an autistic brain. Other brains can navigate on autopilot in most situations and anticipate effortlessly, but autistic brains have to continuously work hard to process and respond to each unique situation. Recharging your battery in time prevents the battery from draining completely.

LIFEHACKS

WHAT YOU CAN DO YOURSELF:

- **6** *Make sure you have a good weekly or monthly plan,* alternating busy days with less busy days.

- **7** *Balance your daily schedule.* Alternate strenuous tasks with tasks that require less effort. Always allow some extra time for strenuous tasks. Time to spare? Then take some rest or do something relaxing.

- **8** *Schedule dedicated rest times.* Plan enough breaks in a day and a week and honor them. For example, set an alarm every hour, get a drink or go to the bathroom.

- **9** *Take time to regulate yourself.* Do things that relax you: walk in nature, listen to music, read a book, watch TV, take a bath ... See also the tips under "Dealing with Sensory Overload" on page 61.

- **10** If work takes a lot of energy from you, *try to maintain a balance between work and your private life.* Define working hours in your schedule and create boundaries. If you work from home, for example, make sure you have a desk that is not part of your private life. A dining table is not a desk.

- **11** *Consider a reduction in working hours* if the work is exhausting, or see if the work can be organized in a less stressful way. Are accommodations available, or is there another way to adjust or adapt your work responsibilities?

- **12** Keep track of your activities for a while and *make a list of things that are energy givers and energy takers.* Perhaps use colors so you can keep a visual distinction between the two. For example, I color walking with the dog yellow (= energy giver), while I color work and social contacts blue (= energy takers). You want your schedule to alternate between energy givers and energy takers as much as possible.

13. Try to make time for your energy givers every day.

14. Give yourself a moment to crash (total recharge moment) after a busy day or after an activity that required a lot of focus and energy. Give yourself time to do nothing, to shut yourself off from the world, or to do something that relaxes you.

15. Allow yourself to cancel an activity if you are no longer enthusiastic about it or if it no longer gives you energy.

WHAT YOU CAN ASK OTHERS TO DO:

- **16** Ask others to help you plan for your needs and ensure you stick to your plan.

- **17** For tasks that are real energy takers for you, ask others for help or if they can take over the task. Examples: calling to make an appointment or cooking. Or ask if they can take over for you when you run out of energy.

- **18** Ask if you are allowed to complete your tasks by breaking them down and completing them one at a time.

- **19** If monitoring your own internal battery alarm is difficult, have others signal you when they see you becoming tired or exhausted.

- **20** Ask to be left alone for a moment when you need to take a break, and ask others not to bombard you with undoubtedly well-intentioned questions about how you feel.

- **21** If you find it difficult to organize and come up with your own relaxing activities, ask someone you trust and like to assist you in developing a list with you. They could even join you in participating in your energy givers (such as sports or walking in nature).

SETTING BOUNDARIES AND DARING TO SAY NO

Many people with autism do not want to be a burden to others, and most do their utmost to meet expectations. Because many things require more energy for autistic people, non-autistic people sometimes overstep their boundaries. Autistic people may have difficulty recognizing their own boundaries, clearly expressing them to others, or saying no in a way that doesn't come across as rude or selfish.

LIFEHACKS

WHAT YOU CAN DO YOURSELF:

22 Try to get to know your own limits better. Ask yourself the following questions: "What do I find important?" "What works best for me?" "What do I really not like to do?" But also: "How much energy do I have at the moment?"

23 If you don't know whether something will push you beyond your limits because you can't estimate how much something will demand of you, ask for more explanation: "How much time do I need for this?" "Can I decide where and when I do it?"

24 If you want time to think about it, use a standard phrase like, "Let me look into it," or, "Let me think about this." Think about whether it is something you want or can handle yourself. If necessary, consult with someone you trust and who understands you.

25 Dare to say no when you are not sure of your yes. Give yourself time to think about writing down the reason(s) for your no and then share them.

26 Communicate clearly and directly that you don't want something: "I don't want that …"

27 Determine the fixed times you are available and share those times with others: "After 8 pm, I no longer answer emails or messages."

WHAT YOU CAN ASK OTHERS TO DO:

28 Choose a trusted person who can help you honor your boundaries. A trusted person can reflect what they see: "I notice you're quiet. Could it be that ... ?"

29 Always ask others to give you time to think about something they want from you, so you can consider whether saying yes would be overstepping your boundaries.

30 Ask to send non-urgent questions by email instead of calling, and arrange this in advance.

31 Share your schedule with others so they can determine for themselves whether you have time to do something.

DEALING WITH A FULL HEAD

Autistic brains are naturally very insecure about themselves and the world. In order to get an answer to the many questions (What? Who? Where? When? Why? How?), they get a lot of information. Because they do not always feel comfortable with the vague "We'll see," the autistic person may also develop all kinds of scenarios and scripts for future events.

These scripts are usually very detailed and often contain many side streets and alleyways. And in order to be able to predict better, autistic people also keep an eye on all kinds of stimuli and possible changes and store events precisely. This can easily become too much information to handle and can be experienced as a full head or a very busy mind.

LIFEHACKS

WHAT YOU CAN DO YOURSELF:

- **32** **Clear your mind by writing down what's in it** on Post-its, in a book, or with the help of an app.

- **33** **Write down your to-do list and check off what is done.** Bundle on one sheet what is not done yet. That way you have an overview of what still needs your energy and attention.

- **34** **Try to distract your thoughts with an activity that requires your attention** but not (too) much: listen to music or make music yourself, do activities such as painting by numbers, puzzles, origami, or watching TV. Set an alarm for the time you want to stop.

- **35** **Become the manager of your worry department.** Find a regular place to sit when you notice yourself starting to worry. Set a timer and stop worrying when it goes off.

- **36** **If your head is full of emotions**, turn to "Dealing with Your Own Emotions" on page 61.

- **37** **Do something with your hands** when your head is full. That often gives you a satisfied feeling afterward. Tidy up or clean and then sing along to cheerful songs. Another possibility: repair something, sew, knit, garden, origami, etc.

- **38** **Accept that you have a full head.** Try to distance yourself and not fight it. Worrying about it doesn't help.

WHAT YOU CAN ASK OTHERS TO DO:

39 **Ask others to listen to you.** Their tips are certainly welcome, but only when you have indicated that it is quieter in your head.

40 If your busy head is dealing with chaos, **ask someone to help you organize your thoughts,** for example, in a mind map, so you get an overview.

41 **Ask others to plan things at times when your head is not (yet) full.** So no heavy meeting at the end of the day.

42 **Look together with a trusted person at what is giving you a cluttered head.** Indicate where others can help you, for example, by taking over a task, clarifying something and making it predictable, adjusting the planning, etc.

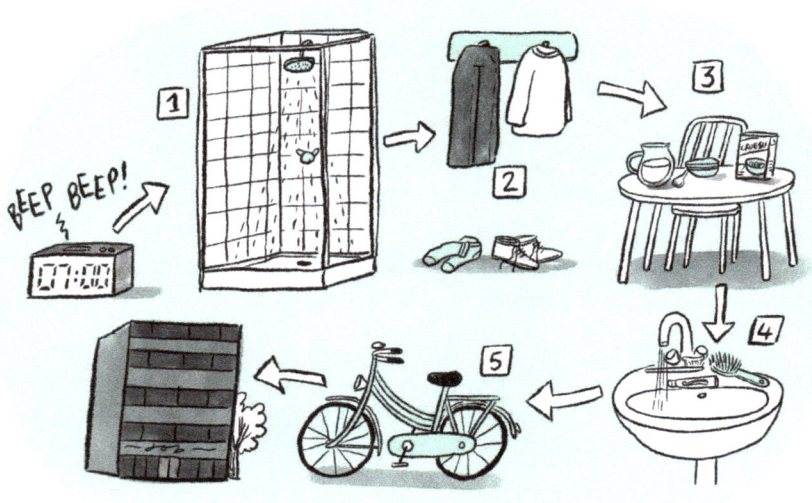

PLANNING AND ORGANIZING

Although people with autism like predictability and structure, planning and organizing can be a major challenge for many. Looking into the future is difficult because many variables are not yet known, and that leads to uncertainty. In addition, many activities that people without autism perform on autopilot require conscious planning from someone with autism.

LIFEHACKS

WHAT YOU CAN DO YOURSELF:

- **43** Set aside space each day for one additional unscheduled task, no more.

- **44** Don't plan too many tasks in one day, and stick to your predetermined schedule as best as possible. There are apps that can help you with better time management.

- **45** Plan for activities that require more of your time and energy than others, such as transitioning between activities, going to the bathroom, organizing your lunch, or getting ready to leave.

- **46** Make lists of the steps in your daily routines and keep track of them. Check off the lists daily. An example of a morning list: get ready, make a lunch box, take the kids to school.

- **47** For recurring activities, note how much time you need to do them. Use a timer if you find it difficult to estimate how long something takes.

- **48** Dare to ask for more time for a task if you notice that you will not meet the deadline.

- **49** Set up fixed routines. For example: lay out your clothes every night for the next day. Perform certain tasks on fixed days. For example: Saturday is washing day and Sunday is ironing day.

WHAT YOU CAN ASK OTHERS TO DO:

50 Ask for activities and their duration to be announced and shared in advance so you can schedule them in a timely manner.

51 Ask others to help you see if your planning is realistic. Have you estimated the time correctly? Is the order of the tasks correct? Ask them to share how they may schedule/plan the activity, because that can inspire you.

52 Ask if someone can make a suggestion for what a plan may look like so you can review it in advance and identify areas that may be difficult for you.

53 Ask your manager to leave flexibility in your schedule for a backup moment. Discuss in advance what you can do during that moment. Finish a task? Relax for a while? Start something new? Also ask if you can keep control over your own schedule.

SATURDAY: WASHING DAY

DEALING WITH YOUR EMOTIONS

A world full of uncertainties, ambiguities, and unpredictability continuously demands a lot of attention from the autistic brain. So much so that sometimes there is little room left to keep a finger on the pulse of what is happening in your inner world: your body signals and the associated emotions.

In this way, one's own emotions, just like the outside world, can become a source of uncertainty or suddenly feel very overwhelming.

LIFEHACKS

WHAT YOU CAN DO YOURSELF:

- **54** **Learn to read your body signals.** Pay special attention to your breathing and heart rate. These can speed up when you get excited. Other body sensations can also help you to know how you feel. For example, when you are anxious, you can get clammy hands, tense muscles, or a headache.

- **55** Keep a journal and **write down what you feel** about different events, situations, people, and places. Use this information to avoid situations or people who make you feel uncomfortable.

56 **Don't be afraid to talk about your emotions.** For example, if you are sad, try to identify what may be causing you to feel that way. If that doesn't work at the moment, come back to it later. This can be done via a message or email.

57 **Communicate honestly about what you feel,** even if you don't know exactly what you feel. Don't say you're fine when you're not feeling well.

58 **Find an outlet for your emotions:** Sing, use a punching bag, listen to music that helps you drain your sadness, work in the garden, etc.

59 **Be gentle with yourself.** Feelings are allowed and okay. It is also okay to feel a little less. You should not feel guilty about having feelings. See also the tips under "Accepting Yourself" on page 113.

60 **It's okay not to know what you're feeling.** If you have trouble distinguishing between emotions, **know that just okay or not okay is also okay.**

WHAT YOU CAN ASK OTHERS TO DO:

- **61** **Share how you want others to support you with your emotions** or during a crash moment. Do you want them to listen to you? To leave you alone? Do you want a hug?

- **62** **Ask others to respect** that you are not feeling well. Search together for a solution that creates space for processing the emotions.

- **63** In case of anger or sadness: **ask to look at the situation together and whether you may have interpreted something differently or incorrectly.** Determine whether you'd like to discuss it further, with no pressure.

- **64** **Ask others how they deal with certain feelings** that you don't know how to deal with. Learn from what others do, and experiment to see if it is something that will work for you too.

- **65** **Let others know they can point out if you look or act stressed**—like frowning, nail-biting, or being extra talkative or really quiet.

- **66** **Ask others to help you regulate when you become upset by a sudden change.** Ask them to leave only when they notice that you have calmed down.

DEALING WITH THE EMOTIONS OF OTHERS

Everyone expresses their emotions in a unique way. These expressions are not always easy to read and predict. That is why it is often a challenge for people with autism to know what others feel or want. Since every person is unique and there are no fixed rules for how to respond to other people's emotions, people with autism are usually very uncertain about how to best handle these situations.

LIFEHACKS

WHAT YOU CAN DO YOURSELF:

67 Consider if you have had a similar experience. This can help you understand the other person's emotions and respond empathetically. For example, have you ever felt sadness yourself? Have you ever experienced the death of a loved one? Experienced disappointment?

68 Share with them if you empathize with similar emotions. Ask if it is okay to tell them about your experience. This will prevent the other person from thinking that you do not want to listen.

69 Soap operas and drama shows on TV often deal with many exaggerated emotions. They can teach you how people react emotionally to situations.

70 Speak up if you don't know how others are feeling or if you're confused by them. For example: "I'm surprised by your reaction. Can you tell me why you're responding the way you are?"

71 Ask questions about emotions. It shows your concern. If someone is crying, ask why they are sad and if there is something you can do to help.

72 If you are overwhelmed by the emotions of others, ask for some time to let it all sink in.

73 If the emotions of others are too intense for you, literally distance yourself and leave the situation. You can explain at a later time the reason you needed to leave.

WHAT YOU CAN ASK OTHERS TO DO:

74 *Ask others to explicitly state how they feel.* They should not expect you to see it yourself.

75 If others want you to understand their feelings, *ask them to explain what they are feeling and where that feeling comes from* in a calm and logical manner.

76 Explain that you do not yet know how best to deal with this. *Ask them to clearly share what they do or do not expect from you.* For example: "Would you like me to only listen to your story? Or would you like me to help you look for possible solutions?"

77 *Ask others to clearly indicate how they want you to respond to their emotions.* Do they want a hug, some space, or no response?

OVERCOMING THE FEAR OF DISAPPOINTING OTHERS

People with autism can often feel very insecure when it comes to sensing what others want or sense. This is something that doesn't come naturally. That insecurity feeds the fear of disappointing others. That fear only grows stronger if they are constantly told that they are acting strangely, reacting inappropriately, or not meeting expectations.

LIFEHACKS

WHAT YOU CAN DO YOURSELF:

- **78** It is good to anticipate what others may expect from you, but do not set the bar too high. Accept that it is not easy for you to estimate what others want from you, and that you may make mistakes in this area.

- **79** View those mistakes as misunderstandings that can be corrected, not as failures.

- **80** If you doubt whether something is good enough, dare to ask.

- **81** Talk about your insecurity. This prevents it from turning into fear.

- **82** If you still feel afraid of disappointing others, express it. Expressing it can reduce your fear because others can then take it into account.

- **83** Just doing your best is often good enough. Sometimes you disappoint others, but know that you did your best. Do your best and forget the rest.

- **84** You can't possibly please everyone. You can't avoid every disappointment. No one can live up to everyone's expectations.

WHAT YOU CAN ASK OTHERS TO DO:

85 **Ask others to be specific about what they expect from you** so you don't have to be unsure whether you are doing it right. For example, if someone expects you to help them, ask for additional details (e.g., what, when, for how long, where, and how).

86 **Ask for honest feedback** when asking if you did a good job.

87 **Ask for interim feedback.** This way you don't have to sit in uncertainty for so long. Also ask for concrete examples if there is something you need to adjust.

88 **Ask for positive feedback** and not just to say something is wrong alongside constructive feedback. What can you do differently, or how do they want you to do something?

Making Choices and Decisions

An autistic brain can react when insecurity occurs, which then can lead to the brain taking in a lot of information or coming up with a lot of scenarios. Making a decision can then become a hellish task. There are many alternatives and many questions to which you cannot get a clear answer in advance. This leads to autism and decision paralysis going hand in hand.

LIFEHACKS

WHAT YOU CAN DO YOURSELF:

- **89** Try to limit your choices to two or three options. This makes choosing easier.

- **90** If there are more than three options and you find it difficult to select three, use a specific system such as "the first three options," "the three cheapest," "the three with the best reviews," etc.

- **91** If someone asks you to choose and you are not ready, ask for time to think about it and say something like, "I'll think about it and get back to you."

- **92** Set yourself some criteria based on things that are important to you. For example, for the purchase of a new phone: price, size, quality of the photos, and the battery. Do the same for the choice of activities and social contacts. For example: what are the important criteria for a good friend?

- **93** Learn to say no in a respectful manner if you feel under pressure to decide or if it is not your preferred choice or the best fit for you.

- **94** Use standard phrases to say no, such as, "It won't work," or, "I don't have time for that."

- **95** Practice those sentences so you can more easily recall them when you need them.

WHAT YOU CAN ASK OTHERS TO DO:

96 **Let people you trust help you make a choice.** Accept their explanation or motivation. Ask them to do the pre-selection and present you with two or three options.

97 **Ask others how they make choices.** What are important criteria for them? Listen to them and talk about it.

98 **Ask for time to make a decision.** What is an easy choice for others may not always be an easy choice for you.

99 **Ask other people to respect your choice,** even if it is not the best choice in their eyes.

SWITCHING FROM ONE THING TO ANOTHER

It is a big misconception that people with autism cannot be flexible. But because an autistic brain has to think about many things consciously, switching quickly from one thing to another is not always as easy as people think it should be. Autism is like driving a car with a manual transmission while everyone else drives an automatic transmission. Even after changing gears many times, the autistic brain may still have to think about changing to a different gear.

LIFEHACKS

WHAT YOU CAN DO YOURSELF:

- (100) Schedule transitions (the gear shifting moments) in your agenda, such as arriving at work or leaving an event.

- (101) During major transitions, take the time to do this step by step, for example, when transitioning from home to work or from being active during the day to sleeping in the evening.

- (102) Use your own "alarms." Use a timer or clock as a tool when you need to switch from one task to another.

- (103) Sometimes it helps to use two timers. One indicates the transition: when you have to stop and start something else. Set the second timer ten minutes earlier than the time you have to transition. That gives you ten minutes of transition time.

- (104) Make checklists that help you move from one task to another. For example, you can't leave the house until you have a cookie and reading material.

- (105) Not sure about the transition time you need? Use a stopwatch to measure the time it takes you to switch from one activity to another, such as changing clothes or checking the contents of your handbag.

- (106) Engage in something that makes waiting easier during switching moments, such as a sudoku or game app.

WHAT YOU CAN ASK OTHERS TO DO:

107 Ask for the start and end times of an activity to be clearly established and shared in advance.

108 If an activity may end sooner or later than originally planned, ask to be given an update on a change in the schedule or timing.

109 Ask others to give you time to transition by announcing the transition moment in advance. For example: "Ten more minutes and then we have to wrap up."

110 Ask others to give you time to do things at your own pace. Ask them to let you work quietly, without interrupting you or asking questions.

DEALING WITH UNPREDICTABLE EVENTS

It's not accurate to say that people with autism don't enjoy variety. An autistic brain likes predictable changes, so it can anticipate things a little more clearly. Events that occur unexpectedly are like a bolt of lightning when there are no clouds in sight. This results in: fright, blind panic, disarray, and losing your true north.

LIFEHACKS

WHAT YOU CAN DO YOURSELF:

- **111** Make the unpredictable a little more predictable. Think through different scenarios in advance. For example, if you have to go somewhere, consider, "What if my travel is delayed? What if public transportation is busier than expected?"

- **112** In addition to what you expect, also consider scenarios B, C, and D and think about what you can do to deal with those scenarios.

- **113** Limit the number of activities that you know may have many unpredictable variables.

- **114** Establish a degree of predictability and routine in your life to avoid being constantly overwhelmed by unforeseen events.

- **115** Try to stay calm in an unpredictable situation. Take a few deep, calming breaths.

116 Notice what others do in that situation and ask them about it too. For example: if a train suddenly stops moving, following the crowd could help you know what to do.

117 Make sure you have a trusted person who can give you tips if you are blocked by a sudden unpredictable event. This can help to make things somewhat predictable again.

118 Schedule time to regroup after unpredictable events.

WHAT YOU CAN ASK OTHERS TO DO:

119 Ask for clear information in advance about what will happen, where, when, how, and why, so you can clarify the specific details and their potential outcomes.

120 If there are variables that may alter a scenario, ask others to indicate the different possibilities in advance. For example: "Grandma is coming over on Sunday, but if she is not feeling well, we will go visit her. We won't know that until Sunday morning."

121 If plans suddenly change, ask others to review the new plans with you. Look for a solution together.

122 If something unpredictable happens, ask the others to clarify not only what is changing, but also what is not changing. For example: "There are more people than expected going to the movies, so we are not going by car but by bus. But the movie we chose is not changing."

123 When others suddenly change something, ask them to explain why they are changing the original plan. For example: on the way home, your partner wants to stop at the store to buy something.

124 Ask others, when they are not sure whether something will occur, to communicate in advance when they will be able to tell you. Ask them to do the same when they do not yet have all the information about a future activity. For example: "We do not yet know whether the meeting will go ahead, but you will get a definite answer tomorrow."

125 Ask the people you live or work with to establish some predictable routines each day so you don't have to be ready for unpredictable moments all day long. This reduces stress and creates a safe environment. Refresh these routines and rituals together over time.

DEALING WITH SENSORY OVERLOAD

The unconscious uncertainty of an autistic brain in combination with a preference for predictability and precision ensures that a person with autism is constantly on the alert. This results in the autistic brain taking in a lot of information, including information that non-autistic brains find irrelevant and often filter out. People with autism want to verify all the details. A brain that is hyperalert not only takes in more stimuli but also reacts more strongly to them. This leads to sensory overload.

LIFEHACKS

WHAT YOU CAN DO YOURSELF:

126 Make your own first aid kit (First Aid for Sensory Overload) that you always have with you. Include items that you can use to survive unpredictable and/or disruptive stimuli: custom earplugs, sunglasses, a fidget spinner or something else to 'fiddle' with ...

127 Determine if there are stimuli you can turn off or reduce. For example, put on your headphones when it's busy or sit in another room.

128 Think of escape scenarios in advance. Where can you go if you get overstimulated? What can you do to help regulate yourself? Who can help you?

129 Try to stay calm and look for ways that may have helped in the past. For example, by doing relaxation breathing (see the all-round toolbox at the beginning of this book (on page 12) or relaxation exercises.

130 Distract your brain by stimulating yourself (with stimming or fidgets) or by doing something that shifts your attention. (For example, find five objects with one-syllable names or close your eyes and think of a pleasant place you recently visited).

131 After the sensory overload, take the time to bring your brain back to a resting state. For example, take a short walk or sit in a quiet place and listen to some soothing music.

132 Try to anticipate unpleasant stimuli you might encounter and prepare yourself for those unpleasant stimuli, such as family parties where you have to give everyone a kiss or a hug. Think in advance about how you want to reduce or avoid those stimuli. For example: say that you prefer shaking hands to a kiss or a hug, or let others know that you will go outside if it gets too busy.

133 When possible, avoid very busy places and times and look for alternatives.

134 At busy events such as a festival, big party or amusement park where you experience many unpredictable stimuli, it is best to discuss with others in advance how long you want to stay. If you are tired from the crowd, ask for a rest and take your sensory overload first aid kit with you.

135 After a day of sensory overload, plan rest to recover from the hustle and bustle. You can also plan rest the day before so that you have enough energy to get through the next day. See also the tips under "Monitoring and Maintaining Energy Balance" on page 15.

WHAT YOU CAN ASK OTHERS TO DO:

136 Ask others to communicate honestly and clearly about possible (unpredictable) stimuli. Whether it will be busy, whether there will be loud music, whether you will have to stand or sit close to each other, etc. Brainstorm possible solutions together.

137 Get permission in advance about using stimulus filters that help to filter stimuli, such as putting on noise-cancelling headphones in the lunchroom at work, going to a designated quiet space, or going outside every now and then.

138 Ask others to make stimuli as predictable as possible. Ask them to check with you in advance about whether you are ready for the stimuli. For example: turning on the bright light at the dentist, the doctor who has to touch you to examine you, entering a noisy room.

139 When you go somewhere for the first time, do some stimulus research beforehand. For example, look at photos of the location on the internet. Then you can see where the speakers are in the restaurant, how close the tables are to each other, where the entrance and exit are, what kind of lighting there is, etc.

140 If you are bothered by busy times at work, ask for a quieter place to work or to work from home part-time.

CONDUCTING CONVERSATIONS

Autistic brains experience more uncertainty than other brains, including the uncertainty of what others may say. This will make it less likely to anticipate, which means that conversations can quickly go too fast or suddenly involve too much information. Conversations are also a challenge because people with autism are often unsure about what they can say or ask in a conversation.

LIFEHACKS

WHAT YOU CAN DO YOURSELF:

141 If you don't know how to greet someone, wait for them to initiate, and copy their greeting behavior. If someone greets you with, "Hey," say, "hey."

142 Determine how you prefer to have conversations: face-to-face, via email, via text or WhatsApp.

143 If you are looking for a starting point in a conversation or want to share less but still show involvement, then make questionnaires in your head. Think in advance about what you know about your conversation partner. Does he or she have children? Does he or she like to go on vacation?

144 In conversations, your own input is not always necessary. Just listening in is also okay. Indicate this with small signals such as, "I understand what you mean."

145 Think of some standard sentences in advance to answer unexpected questions, such as: "I'll think about it and come back to it later." Install your own chatbot (your own artificial intelligence) and think of some standard sentences in advance that you could answer to unexpected questions that you don't immediately know what to do with. Examples:

- You surprised me with your question. I have to think about it for a while and come back to it later.

- I don't have my calendar with me. Can I send you a message to confirm or decline the appointment?

- I don't have an answer to that right now.

146 If you are not sure what your conversation partner means with his or her question, check whether your answer is what he or she expects: "Does this answer your question?"

147 It's okay to ask additional questions, and don't be afraid to ask the wrong question. Use I-statements if you didn't understand something and want more explanation. For example: "I'm not sure I understand. Can you explain it again?"

WHAT YOU CAN ASK OTHERS TO DO:

- (148) Let others know that you appreciate sincere, honest questions and that socially acceptable questions and small talk are not your thing.

- (149) Clear, concrete, and open communication works best. The rule, "Do what you say and say what you do," also applies. Comments with multiple meanings are best avoided. Underlying messages are also best made explicit, because it is often difficult for you to read between the lines.

- (150) Indicate that the tone of voice, facial expressions, and body language can be confusing to you. Your uncertainty makes you easily doubt the other person's intentions.

- (151) When talking, don't sit across from each other, but at a 90-degree angle. This way, you're less distracted by someone's body language, and you don't have to look at each other directly.

- (152) Share if you think someone is talking too much or too long or not getting to the point. Say that you are bothered by too much information.

- (153) Express that you appreciate others starting a conversation or asking you a question if you are alone or find it difficult to start a conversation. Often, you want to start a conversation with others, but you just don't know how to do that.

BUILDING AND MAINTAINING CLOSE RELATIONSHIPS

Most people with autism have an authentic longing for close relationships, such as friendship or an intimate partner relationship. At the same time, close relationships are even more challenging than superficial and professional contacts: the closer the relationship, the fewer fixed and explicit rules there are. For the absolute thinkers that people with autism are, the unwritten and relative rules of close relationships are often a mystery or a confusing tangle.

LIFEHACKS

WHAT YOU CAN DO YOURSELF:

154 **Compare having close relationships to having plants.** One needs it, the other doesn't. **If you need close relationships, give them nourishment and attention.** Reach out and contact your friends to meet up.

155 **Friendship is give and take.** You will have to do some things that the other person likes to do that you may not like or enjoy. There should also be a balance in treating or exchanging gifts.

156 **Don't expect to find everything you need in one person.** You can walk well with one friend, talk well with another. Even an intimate partner can't give you everything you need. So you don't have to do everything together with a friend or partner.

157 **Dare to cross the threshold of the first contact and make an appointment.** A first contact is quite exciting for many. Keep the meeting short and link it to a concrete activity such as a visit to a museum you know one hour before closing time. That way you don't have to talk the whole time. There is already something to talk about, and you know how long the contact will last.

158 **Remember that with real friends, you should be able to be yourself and talk freely.** If not, then they are acquaintances or conversation partners.

159 For some, it is enough to have one or two best friends by their side. Others do not find anyone they click with and have no friends. That is also completely okay, and therefore you are not necessarily lonely.

160 All relationships have a beginning and an end. Friendships can fizzle out. That doesn't necessarily have to do with autism.

161 Attach importance to your own well-being. A social life ultimately brings with it a lot of obligations and pressure. Weigh the pros and cons for yourself and think about what you want for yourself.

WHAT YOU CAN ASK OTHERS TO DO:

162 If you find it difficult to initiate contact, let others know that they should not expect it from you often. It is important to let others know that you appreciate being invited.

163 After an activity or evening, clearly agree on who will contact you next time and when. This does not have to be done immediately, because social contacts require a lot of energy, but plan this for the future.

164 Let others know that you will choose whether or not to accept an invitation. This way you ensure that others do not fill this in for you, for example, that they do not invite you because they think people with autism do not like parties.

165 Indicate that your rejection of an invitation is not a personal rejection. Sometimes it just doesn't work out or you simply don't have the energy left for an activity with friends.

166 If there are certain expectations associated with a certain situation, ask them to make these expectations known. If someone invites you to a joint activity and there are expectations associated with this, ask them to communicate these clearly in advance. For example: they expect you to help pay for the bill at a restaurant.

SURVIVING PARTIES

Most people with autism don't like improvised gatherings and parties. Too many (unpredictable) stimuli (a balloon that bursts usually does not warn), very few fixed procedures, unknown people, the unpredictable physical proximity of others, not to mention the touching (kissing, dancing, hugging...), and—last but not least—the implicit and vague social rules. Autistic people festively decline all these things.

LIFEHACKS

WHAT YOU CAN DO YOURSELF:

- **167** **Decide in advance what kind of parties you want to go to.** Give yourself permission to make the choices that are right for you.

- **168** If you get tired or overstimulated during a meeting, *take a break or step away for a while.* Afterward, explain why this was necessary. For example, bring a pair of headphones or something that relaxes you. See also the tips under "Dealing with Sensory Overload" on page 61.

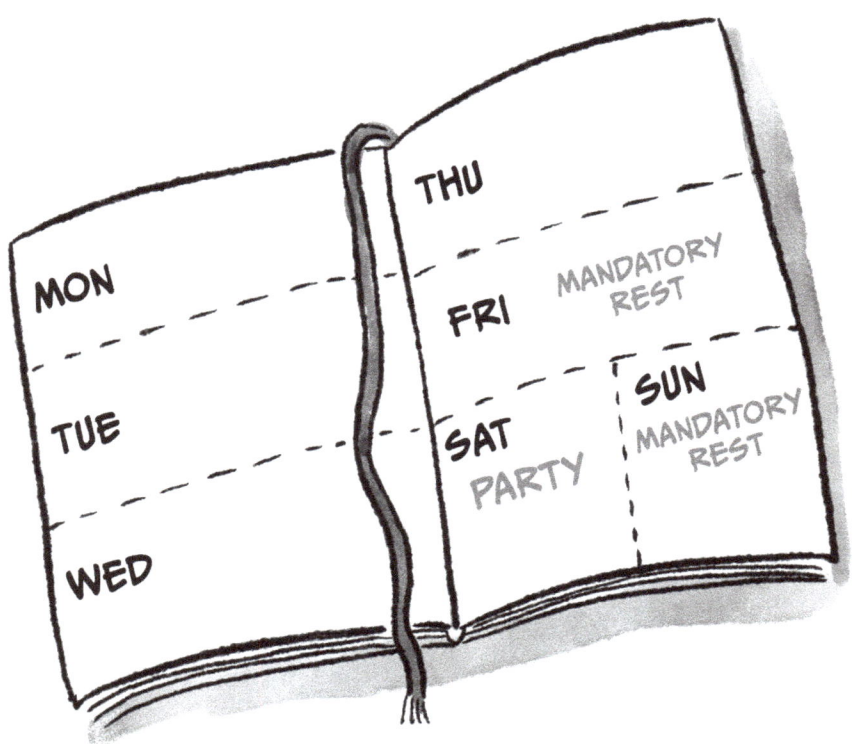

169 Ask questions to the party organizer in advance if you are nervous. Also try to find out what social rules apply. For example, do you have to bring a gift?

170 Make sure you arrive first at a party, not last. That way you avoid having to greet everyone.

171 If you like to escape the social chatter, it can help to have a task to perform during the party or activity: taking photos, making snacks, etc.

172 If the party is at your home, make to-do lists in advance that you can check off. Also ask for help before and during the party.

173 Choose comfortable party clothes so you are not bothered by itchy glitter, for example.

174 If you fear that you won't be able to last (long) at a party, avoid driving to the party with others so you don't have to wait for others to go home or you don't have to cut short others' fun.

175 Spread your visits and social activities during busy festive periods. This way, the entire month of January is good for New Year's greetings.

WHAT YOU CAN ASK OTHERS TO DO:

176 Ask others to provide sufficient explanation about the party in advance. Who will be there? What is on the agenda? What's there to eat?

177 Indicate that you do not want to be forced to participate in something you do not feel like doing, such as board games or dancing. Explain that you enjoy watching.

178 Share in advance that you do not know how long you will stay. Ask for understanding if you wish to leave early.

179 Brainstorm in advance about a place where you can go if it is too busy or if you want peace. To the garden? To a separate room?

180 Challenge others to go outside the usual scenarios. For example, parties don't always have to be in the evening. During the day can also be an option.

SLEEPING WELL

Sensory overload, uncertainty, worrying about what happened, going through twelve scenarios about what still needs to happen... A brain that is constantly running at full capacity can hardly find and keep peace. For autistic brains, life is anything but sleep-inducing. Scientific research shows that sleep problems are one of the most common complaints of people with autism.

LIFEHACKS

WHAT YOU CAN DO YOURSELF:

- **181** **Find out what good sleep is.** Find out how much sleep you need and take that into account. Not everyone needs to sleep eight hours a day. It is also normal to only fall asleep after half an hour (or an hour for the elderly) or to wake up a few times during the night. How well you sleep is often more important than how long you sleep.

- **182** **Make sure your room is clean and quiet.** No clutter, no TV or other screens, no piles of books on (bedside) tables.

183 Provide fixed sleep rituals and go to bed at a fixed time. Stop looking at screens half an hour before bedtime.

184 Make yourself unreachable for phone calls or messages from a certain time (for example, after 8:00 PM), and let others know this is a boundary for you.

185 Find ways to clear your mind before you go to bed. Write things down in a notebook, build with LEGOs, listen to music, etc.

186 Change your sheets at least once every two weeks and wash your nightwear every three to four days. This is not only good for your health (less bacteria), but it also helps you sleep better.

187 Look for something that can help calm you if you have trouble falling asleep: a weighted blanket, a cherry stone pillow, body socks, etc.

188 Focus on your breathing before going to sleep, for example, by saying a mantra and doing a breathing exercise at the same time (see the all-round toolbox at the front of this book on page 11).

189 If you wake up earlier than usual, don't force yourself to go back to sleep. Get up and do something that will help you start your day off right. Maybe you can do something early in the morning that will shorten that annoying to-do list, or complete a task that you've been putting off for a long time.

WHAT YOU CAN ASK OTHERS TO DO:

- **190** Point out that sometimes you need more sleep than others, but sometimes you need much less.

- **191** It helps if there is understanding for your sleep difficulties, which can sometimes make you less focused at work, arrive late, or need more breaks.

- **192** Ask others not to show disappointment, because that will make you feel guilty. Find a solution together for the missed tasks or meeting.

- **193** Discuss with your partner what you need to sleep better. There is nothing wrong with sleeping separately. One person has a different sleep ritual or rhythm than the other. You may be a better partner after a good night's sleep.

ENJOYING MEALS

For most people, meals are pleasant moments that their brains can easily digest. You don't really have to think about it, with a bit of luck it's nutritious and tasty, and you can socialize at the same time. That's not the case for a lot of people with autism. Eating requires more organization of their brains. The social aspect of eating together is a form of multitasking that demands a lot from an autistic brain. And there are the strong reactions to smells, tastes, or certain textures. Mealtime does not give energy, but demands it. Yet mealtimes are important for many people with autism because they provide structure to the day as anchor points.

LIFEHACKS

WHAT YOU CAN DO YOURSELF:

- **194** If it takes a lot of energy to prepare meals, cook for several meals at once and put separate portions in your freezer. That way you only have to take out what you need to warm up.

- **195** During busy periods, accept comfort food or a sandwich instead of a hot meal.

- **196** Try to ensure a healthy diet with sufficient variation.

- **197** Get to know your own food sensitivities and adjust your menu accordingly. It is not a problem if a dish that is easy to eat returns regularly on the menu, as long as it's not every day. (See previous tip.)

- **198** Make a weekly menu for your hot meals and determine in advance what you will eat every day. This way you "force" yourself to eat healthy and varied foods.

- **199** In addition, a weekly menu also helps to bundle your groceries, for example, on one (fixed) day of the week.

- **200** If you are eating alone at home, turn on the TV or music. This gives you the feeling that you are not alone and makes eating more enjoyable.

WHAT YOU CAN ASK OTHERS TO DO:

201 Ask others if they can cook something extra for you now and then.

202 If you are invited to dinner, ask them to tell you in advance what is on the menu and whether you are expected to bring anything (drinks, dessert, etc.).

203 If you would like to bring (part of) your food for yourself or for others, say so in advance. Make it clear that you do not like to deviate from your eating habits or have aversions or allergies to certain foods or textures. You can also suggest cooking for the other(s).

204 Share your dietary preferences and recipes you enjoy. This increases the chance that they will be on the menu. Please give positive feedback if you like the food.

COPING WITH LOSS

Whether it is a person, a pet, an object, a job, or health, loss is a major challenge for most people. This challenge is even greater for people with autism, because loss always brings changes in routines. And when the loss is sudden and unpredictable, someone with autism cannot prepare for those changes. In addition, loss usually causes a lot of (intense) emotions, and dealing with one's own emotions is a challenge in itself for people with autism. Therefore, see also the tips under "Dealing with Your Own Emotions" on page 33.

LIFEHACKS

WHAT YOU CAN DO YOURSELF:

205 *Acknowledge and allow your own feelings.* All feelings are okay and are allowed to be there. Even if you don't feel anything, that's okay. People with autism can react very differently to loss. Give yourself time to grieve, and don't compare yourself to others. Sometimes, the emotions don't impact you right away and sneak up on you later when you least expect it.

206 Dealing with loss can be compared to paddling a rowing boat. If you can only think about how it used to be, you will continue to row with one paddle: the loss paddle. If you do not dwell on this loss, you will only row with the recovery paddle. Then your boat will go in circles. *Only with two paddles will your boat move forward.*

207 Plan in advance what you are going to do on days of great loss, such as a birthday, New Year, All Saints' Day and All Souls' Day, an anniversary of a death, etc.

208 Set up a mourning corner at home. Decorate it with things that evoke beautiful memories.

209 Keep the memory alive and do something that brings back positive memories. For example, prepare your deceased mother's favorite recipe or make a painting of your deceased pet.

210 Focus on who or what you still have or what you still can do.

211 Look at your schedule to see what changes will occur due to the loss. Look for alternatives for losses, whether it's a canceled activity due to illness or the absence of a colleague after a job loss.

WHAT YOU CAN ASK OTHERS TO DO:

212 Explain how you cope with loss, and ask others to honor your process. For example, just because you don't express your emotions doesn't mean you don't have them.

213 If your grief and sorrow are slow to develop, ask others to check in with you after a longer period of time to see how you are doing.

214 Ask for a space at work where you can be alone if things are tough.

215 Explain that you don't always have the energy to ask for practical help, like making food, or don't know who to ask for something. Let people know that you appreciate it when others suggest help.

216 If others want to offer you hope and perspective, think together about what might help you. For example, does it help you to plan a mourning period with a fixed end date? Or for people to express positive affirmations when you can't do it yourself, such as "You will overcome this"?

BOOSTING YOUR NEGATIVE OR LOW SELF-ESTEEM

For people with autism, it is not always as obvious how to do certain things as quickly, effortlessly, or successfully as people without autism. Comparison to others often tilts to the negative side: "I can't do it as well, as quickly, or as smoothly as the others." Being positive about yourself and staying that way then becomes a major challenge.

LIFEHACKS

WHAT YOU CAN DO YOURSELF:

- **217** Every day, reflect on the successes you have achieved, even if many things did not go as planned. Visualize them (literally). Start with the small successes, for example, that you still managed to go to bed on time. Then take a picture of the clock.

- **218** Tell yourself regularly that you are good (enough). Hang these affirmations up so you can read them regularly: "I am good enough," or, "I gave my very best." Maybe stick this on the mirror in your bathroom so you are reminded of it every day.

- **219** Accept and collect compliments. For every negative comment you receive, you need to receive three positive ones to keep your self-esteem up. Write down all the compliments you receive, save them, and read them often.

220 Use a "pride diary" in which you write down something you are proud of every evening, for example, that you have cleaned your bathroom or gave up your seat on the bus to an older person. Read it again regularly.

221 Find out what your own strengths are and use them as much as possible. That is what the ambassadors who contributed to this book did. (See pages 118–124.) Make a list of them and do something with them, such as trying out a new hobby or helping others with something you are good at, such as repairing something.

222 Do what you like to do and what fills you up. That will make success more regular.

223 Compare yourself to yesterday, last week, and last month. Don't compare yourself to others. Look at the path you've already taken and what is working for you now.

WHAT YOU CAN ASK OTHERS TO DO:

- **224** **Ask others to give you positive feedback regularly.** Ask them to be honest, clear and transparent.

- **225** **Ask those around you to read more about autism** so they understand that what comes easily for others actually requires a lot of effort from you. Let them know it would be nice if you got compliments for that.

- **226** **Ask not to use the sandwich method for feedback:** first a compliment, then criticism, and finally a positive ending. People with autism tend to remember only the negative.

- **227** **Ask for solution-oriented feedback,** to clearly state what is going well and to give concrete tips on what can be improved. See also the tips under "Overcoming the Fear of Disappointing Others" on page 43.

BEING ABLE TO BE YOURSELF IN CONNECTION WITH OTHERS

Because their brains work differently, people with autism sometimes react unusually in the eyes of others. They may also need things that non-autistic people don't usually need–for example, needing to know everything in advance, including every last detail. But autism is not always visible to the environment. Because they want to meet expectations and because they want to belong, people with autism sometimes hide their authentic selves and mask their autism. They then risk losing their authenticity and their ability to be themselves. On the other hand, no one can be themselves always and everywhere. Occasionally, doing something for someone else that goes against your own nature and needs strengthens the relationship and increases the chance of connection. People with autism find it more difficult to find this balance. It also costs them more energy.

LIFEHACKS

WHAT YOU CAN DO YOURSELF:

228 Find out what you need at a minimum to be able to be yourself. Share that with the people you live or work with.

229 Establish your boundaries. See also the tips under "Setting Boundaries and Daring to Say No" on page 21.

230 Surround yourself with people who accept you as you are, even if they sometimes ask for something of you that is more difficult for you. In a good relationship, each partner lets the other be themselves as much as possible and takes into account the individuality and needs of the other.

231 Make sure there are enough situations where you dare to be yourself. Plan enough activities where you don't have to mask your autism. Some people participate in activities for and by people with autism, because they can be themselves there among like-minded people.

232 Get inspired by the "life hacks" of people with autism to be more themselves. For example, if you want to participate but don't like to be around a lot of people, you might ask, "I want to participate in the project, but is it okay if I attend the meetings online instead of in person?' Or if you don't like small talk, you can eat an apple during a break, because no one expects you to talk with your mouth full.

233 Sometimes people with autism mistakenly think that others expect something from them. If you are not completely sure, ask the other person what he or she expects from you.

234 Meeting the other person's needs doesn't necessarily have to be at your own expense. Explain that you want to meet their expectations, but ask if you can do it your way. For example: "I want to come to your party, but is it okay if I come a little later (or leave early)?"

WHAT YOU CAN ASK OTHERS TO DO:

235 Ask for respect for your choices, your way of thinking, and your way of being. Often you do things because it brings you peace, gives you energy, or makes the situation manageable.

236 Clarify your own behavior to other people. Why do you do something or not? This increases the chance that the other person will show understanding.

237 Ask for clear and transparent communication of expectations. This will prevent you from making efforts that are not expected of you or from masking unnecessarily.

238 Entice others to learn more about autism. Hand out the "Autism Friendliness" pocket book or poster (made by Strengthmakers *in* Autism). Or suggest organizing an autism immersion session or an autism experience circuit at work or in the neighborhood.

ACCEPTING YOURSELF

According to scientific research, people with autism are particularly critical of themselves, even more critical than people without autism. Their absolute thinking also sets the bar high for themselves. The fact that many things are more difficult for them than for others and that the environment does not always show the necessary understanding for this makes it a challenge for people with autism to like themselves.

LIFEHACKS

WHAT YOU CAN DO YOURSELF:

- **239** Don't set the bar too high for yourself. It doesn't have to be 100% good, 75% is also good. This simple rule can be applied in many situations.

- **240** Nobody is perfect. And everyone makes mistakes. Learning to embrace your own imperfections makes living with autism a lot easier.

- **241** Don't ignore your mistakes and failures, but be gentle with yourself when you encounter them.

- **242** If you are critical of yourself, give constructive criticism and formulate it in terms of possible growth. Try saying, for example, "I'm learning a lot about small talk," not, "I'm not good at small talk."

- **243** Focus on what works and not just on what doesn't. For example, if you can't work full-time, try working part-time or doing volunteer work. That way you can still say that you work. The same goes for sports: if team sports are too difficult, try to do sports alone. That way you remain a sporty person.

- **244** Try to be grateful for what does work out.

- **245** Loving yourself takes time and practice. Be patient and don't give up if it doesn't work right away.

WHAT YOU CAN ASK OTHERS TO DO:

246 *If you are doing something that you find difficult, name it* and talk about it with others.

247 *Work together to find a compromise* that works for everyone.

248 *Ask others to correct you* when you make a negative statement about yourself. So if you say, "I'll never succeed," the other can correct you with, "Never say never. You've gotten this far. That alone deserves a medal."

249 An important element of self-acceptance is knowing that you are not the only one for whom life is not a bed of roses. So *surround yourself with people who talk openly about their limitations and shortcomings.*

AT THE BEGINNING OF THIS BOOK YOU READ FIVE ALL-ROUND TIPS.
HERE YOU GET AN EXTRA ALL-ROUND TIP ON TOP. (THAT MAKES 250 TIPS IN TOTAL!)

USE YOUR STRENGTHS AND INTERESTS

This book is about common challenges for people with autism. About what can be difficult or tricky for them. About challenges and obstacles they encounter.

Know that autism also has another side. Absolute thinking and a sense of precision help people with autism excel in certain things, such as remembering dates and facts, noticing details, following rules, etc. Autistic people often have an incredibly strong sense of justice. Because they think differently, they often come up with unusual and creative solutions. They don't need brainstorming sessions to think outside the box, simply because with their neurodivergent brains, they were never in the box to begin with. And they sometimes know a lot about certain subjects.

Every person with autism also has strengths and talents apart from the autism characteristics. Get to know your strengths, appreciate them, and especially look at how you can use them in things that are sometimes difficult.

The ambassadors and authors who collaborated on this book have already done the exercise. Here they list their strengths. Hopefully this will inspire you to do the same.

PETER VERMEULEN

Peter has been working extensively with autism for almost forty years. He has written several books on autism and gives lectures all over the world. He lives with his wife and two lovely dogs and is the proud grandfather of four amazing grandsons.

He enjoys cycling, reading, film, and music.

Strengths:

- Strong in empowering people with autism.

- Good at pretending to be confident, even when I'm not. I use that strength when I want to give peace to people with autism who are even more insecure than I am.

- Can explain autism well.

- Sense of humor, even when things are tough. I use that strength to learn to accept myself. By laughing at myself, I put my limitations into perspective.

CHRISTOPHER VAN ROY

Christopher is an educational psychologist and has a postgraduate degree in business management. He has been working with people with autism for over eighteen years. He himself was diagnosed in 2014. He started as a supervisor for children and young people with autism in a summer camp. Christopher has been working at the Flemish Autism Association since 2023, where he supports volunteers and policymaking. Additionally, since 2023, he has been an autism consultant via ekseko.be, which provides support to people with autism, helps employers with their questions, and provides training on autism. He has two lovely children: Thimo and Willow. They mean everything to him.

Strengths:

- Strong in analyzing the situation or task in order to arrive at an efficient approach.

- Strong in explaining and making people understand autism.

- Unfortunately strong in camouflaging, but fortunately also in dealing with social expectations and social situations.

- Sense of humor. That way I can make difficult moments a little easier and bring back positivity.

AN VANDERSTRAETEN

An is a clerk and study tutor. She lives alone with two cats but can always go visit with her twin sister. She likes climbing, crocheting, gymnastics, photography, and skiing.

Strengths:

- Structuring and analytical thinking. I use these strengths when I am faced with choices or have to deal with sudden changes.

- Capturing the souls of people in photos. That is what I use to keep myself busy during parties and gatherings.

JESSICA LANDUYT

Jessica is a cleaning employee at the AZ Maria Middelares hospital in Ghent. She lives with her boyfriend Tim and her border collie Nala. She is also a proud godmother.

Her hobbies include cooking and baking, walking and spinning.

She is an ambassador for Strengthmakers *in* Autism because she believes it is important to educate society even more about autism.

Strengths:

- Always ready to help others.

- A go-getter: if I want to achieve something, I give it my all, even if it is sometimes difficult. I keep going until my goal is reached.

- I keep challenging myself and don't always choose the easy way with a lot of structure. For example, I chose a work location where you don't know in advance how many rooms you have to clean per day.

- Eye for detail: I see things that other people don't see. For example, I immediately notice when a colleague is wearing new glasses, while for others it can take days.

- I dare to stand up for myself and do something new.

MARCIA VERHULST

Marcia is an independent psychologist. She works mainly with people with autism. Marcia also gives training courses in which she uses the Autism Experiencing Circuit (developed by Strengthmakers *in* Autism), according to recent insights about the predictive brain in autism.

Her hobbies include walking her dog Unit, cross-training, and going to heavy metal festivals.

Her dog Unit also functions as an assistance dog and is an important pillar and co-therapist in providing therapy.

Strengths:

— Strong in listening, which helps me do my job as a psychologist well.

— Animal lover, which helps me to make contacts with others.

— Open, honest, and curious, which is why I like to take on new challenges.

— A go-getter.

— Trust and authenticity are very important to me.

EVI TROCH

Evi is an ambassador for Strengthmakers *in* Autism. In daily life, she is a housewife. She lives with her partner, their fourteen-year-old daughter, a small dog, and a large rabbit. She likes mini-series and films, walking, and reading.

Strengths:

- I am social and need social contacts to feel good. I use that when I want to build and maintain close relationships.

- My job as a housewife and my ambassadorship ensure that I can monitor my energy balance very well. If I ever push my limits, I can quickly build in more rest and relaxation.

- I am eager to learn and enjoy doing new things.

AND THE LAST AMBASSADOR

Finally, there is another ambassador of Strengthmakers *in* Autism who prefers to remain anonymous, but whom we would still like to thank.

Dear you, you know which person with autism I am talking about. Thank you for sharing your expertise, experiences, and tips in this book. They are also invaluable to us.

STRENGTHMAKERS *IN* AUTISM

Strengthmakers *in* Autism wants to make everyone who strives for full inclusion of people with autism stronger in that ambition. And by everyone, we literally mean everyone: people with autism, parents and family members, professionals, policy makers, politicians, and all people who want to make their company, organization, or association autism-friendly.

As long as inclusion is a goal and not a reality, we will stubbornly and determinedly continue with what we have been doing for over thirty years: empowering people and organizations with a heart for autism in autism and autism friendliness. We deploy a wide range of empowering activities: we raise awareness, inspire, inform, connect people, and get them moving.

We do this for and with people with autism. Because we believe that we can only achieve this inclusion together.

And we can use everyone, including you, the reader of this book. We would like to make you strong in autism!

ALSO BY PETER VERMEULEN

What Really Works for Children with Autism is a practical guide in which you discover what exactly autism is, the ten most important needs of these children, and how you can support them in this. The book offers concrete tools and simple strategies so you as a (grand)parent, teacher, therapist, or (co)supervisor can learn to deal with these children differently and better.

ALSO BY PETER VERMEULEN

A Mom's Choice Award winner, ***Autism as Context Blindness*** provides a unique glance into the minds of individuals with autism. Full of often humorous examples, the book examines context as it relates to perception, social interaction, communication, and knowledge. The book concludes with a section on how to address contextual sensitivity—a skill vital for successful functioning.

Did you like this book?

Rate it and share your opinion!

amazon.com

Not what you expected? Tell us!

Most negative reviews occur when the book did not reach expectation. Did the description build any expectations that were not met? Let us know how we can do better.

Please drop us a line at info@fhautism.com.
Thank you so much for your support!

www.ingramcontent.com/pod-product-compliance
Lightning Source LLC
Jackson TN
JSHW081056150126
96817JS00007B/11